Science

YEAR 4

Answers

Sue Hunter

Jenny Macdonald

GALORE PARK

AN HACHETTE UK COMPANY

Every effort has been made to trace all copyright holders, but if any have been inadvertently overlooked, the Publishers will be pleased to make the necessary arrangements at the first opportunity.

Although every effort has been made to ensure that website addresses are correct at time of going to press, Galore Park cannot be held responsible for the content of any website mentioned in this book. It is sometimes possible to find a relocated web page by typing in the address of the home page for a website in the URL window of your browser.

Hachette UK's policy is to use papers that are natural, renewable and recyclable products and made from wood grown in sustainable forests. The logging and manufacturing processes are expected to conform to the environmental regulations of the country of origin.

Orders: please contact Bookpoint Ltd, 130 Milton Park, Abingdon, Oxon OX14 4SB. Telephone: (44) 01235 827720. Fax: (44) 01235 400454. Email education@bookpoint.co.uk. Lines are open from 9 a.m. to 5 p.m., Monday to Saturday, with a 24-hour message answering service. Visit our website at www.galorepark.co.uk for details of other revision guides for Common Entrance, examination papers and Galore Park publications.

ISBN: 978 1 4718 5634 1

© Sue Hunter and Jenny Macdonald 2015

First published in 2015 by

Galore Park Publishing Ltd,

An Hachette UK Company

Carmelite House

50 Victoria Embankment

London EC4Y 0DZ

www.galorepark.co.uk

Impression number 10 9 8 7 6 5 4 3 2 1

Year 2019 2018 2017 2016 2015

Typeset in India by Aptara, Inc.

Printed in the UK

A catalogue record for this title is available from the British Library.

About the authors

Sue Hunter has been a science teacher in a variety of schools for more years than she cares to remember. Her experiences have included teaching in a choir school and a local authority middle school, teaching GCSE and A level in the Netherlands and a short spell as a full-time mother of two. She was Head of Science at St Hugh's School in Oxfordshire until her recent retirement and is a member of the Common Entrance setting team. She has run a number of training courses for prep school teachers, including at Malvern College and for the Independent Association of Preparatory Schools (IAPS), and is currently IAPS Subject Leader for science and a member of the Independent Schools Inspectorate. She has also served for a number of years as a governor of local primary schools.

Jenny Macdonald has been a teacher for many years, teaching in both state and private schools. For the last 15 years she has been teaching science at St Hugh's School in Oxfordshire. She moved to Oxfordshire in the 1970s and has always enjoyed outdoor pursuits, having raised three children and countless chickens, sheep and dogs on the family smallholding. She is chairman of a local choral society, sings in a variety of local choirs, and would like to have more time to relax in the chairs that she enjoys re-upholstering.

Contents

Introduction

About this book

Science is a subject that invites enquiry. The text in *Science Year 4* contains many interesting facts and opens the way for further research should a child feel inclined to find out more. Each chapter includes a number of exercises that are designed to focus the readers' attention on what they have read, assess their understanding of the material and to encourage them to think more analytically about the topic. There are a number of different types of exercise, e.g. cloze ('fill in the gaps') exercises, comprehension type questions and extension exercises requiring thought and application. All can be used in a number of ways depending on the ability of the pupils and the requirements of a lesson. The extension exercises, for example, could be used by teachers as stimuli for discussion, homework activities, opportunities for further development for quick workers, etc.

The answers given here should be seen as a guide. We do not expect every child to reproduce our answers exactly and each child should be encouraged to respond to the best of their ability. For some, success will be achieved if they can correctly extract basic information from the text. Others can be encouraged to look for more than the most basic answer by reading the text more critically. Those with the ability and interest can be encouraged to find out more and expand their knowledge through further reading or to think more deeply about the implications and applications of the material offered.

Sue Hunter and Jenny Macdonald

August 2015

The variety of living things

This chapter covers the following elements of the National Curriculum for Year 4.

Pupils should be taught to:

● recognise that living things can be grouped in a variety of ways
● explore and use classification keys to help group, identify and name a variety of living things in their local and wider environment.

It also includes the following elements not mentioned in the National Curriculum (ISEB 1b):

● how vertebrates can be divided into fish, amphibians, reptiles, birds and mammals, and invertebrates into snails and slugs, worms, spiders and insects
● how plants can be divided into flowering plants (including grasses) and non-flowering plants such as ferns and mosses.

Activities in this chapter offer opportunities to work scientifically by:

● making systematic and careful observations
● gathering, recording, classifying and presenting data in a variety of ways to help in answering questions
● recording findings using simple scientific language, drawings and labelled diagrams.

Exercise 1.1

1 mouse – mammal

2 tree frog – amphibian

3 polar bear – mammal

4 boa constrictor – reptile

5 golden eagle – bird

6 shark – fish

7 turtle – reptile

8 natterjack toad – amphibian

9 tuna – fish

10 penguin – bird

Exercise 1.2

● **insects**   animals with an exoskeleton and six legs
● **spiders**   animals with an exoskeleton and four pairs of legs
● **worms**   animals with soft bodies that are long, thin and flexible
● **slugs and snails** animals with soft bodies that slither along on their stomachs

Exercise 1.3a

1 millions, groups, study

2 skeleton, vertebrates, invertebrates

3 five, mammals, amphibians, reptiles

4 exoskeleton, insects, spiders

5 slugs, snails, snails, predators

6 flowering, insects, wind, mosses

Exercise 1.3b: extension

1 (a) ladybird

  (b) cat

  (c) slug

  (d) house spider (spider)

  (e) earthworm

2
ladybird	insect
cat	mammal
slug	invertebrate (gastropod)
house spider	spiders
earthworm	invertebrate (segmented worm)

3 Check pupils' ideas. Are their descriptions clear enough with the correct details for identification? Are other pupils able to identify the animals and say which groups they belong in?

Exercise 1.4

1 A oak

  B horse chestnut

  C elder

  D field maple

  E beech

2 A fly agaric

  B shaggy ink cap

  C the sickener

  D parasol mushroom

  E sulphur tuft

2 Caring for the environment

This chapter covers the following elements of the National Curriculum for Year 4.

Pupils should be taught to:

● recognise that environments can change and that this can sometimes pose dangers to living things.

It also includes the following elements not mentioned in the National Curriculum:

● that life processes occur in familiar animals and plants and how these are determined by the habitats in which they are found (ISEB 1c)
● how living things, e.g. pets, farm animals, wildlife found in parks and gardens and the associated plant life, carry out these life processes within their respective habitats (ISEB 1c)
● how examples of human actions (both positive and negative) affect the environment (ISEB 1d)
● about the need to protect and conserve living things and their environment, e.g. endangered species, effects of pollution, habitat destruction (ISEB 1e).

Activities in this chapter offer opportunities to work scientifically by:

● setting up simple practical enquiries
● making systematic and careful observations
● gathering, recording, classifying and presenting data in a variety of ways to help in answering questions
● recording findings using simple scientific language
● reporting on findings from enquiries, including oral and written explanations, and displays
● identifying differences, similarities or changes related to simple scientific ideas and processes
● using results to draw simple conclusions, make predictions for new values, suggest improvements and raise further questions.

Exercise 2.1

1 The surroundings or the whole of the natural world.

2 habitat

3 food and water, oxygen, shelter and a place to breed

4 Any three from: movement, reproduction, nutrition, growth, (respiration, sensitivity, excretion).

Exercise 2.2a

1 Answers will depend on the environment around the school. Accept any two appropriate ways in which human activity has changed the environment near the school.

2 Putting things into the environment that should not be there.

3 Burning fuels such as coal, oil or gas; dumping rubbish; materials from factories leaking into the environment. (Accept any one appropriate suggestion of a source of pollution.)

4 tiger, lemur, snow leopard, otter (Accept any two appropriate suggestions of species endangered through habitat loss.)

5 endangered

6 Conserve remaining habitat, restore habitat, captive breeding and reintroduction.

7 They might become extinct.

Exercise 2.2b

1 pollution

2 habitat, destroyed, rubbish

3 endangered

4 extinct

5 habitat

Exercise 2.2c: extension

The poster should show an understanding of the environmental problems of rubbish dumping. It should be persuasive, neat, clear and eye-catching. It might include alternatives to dumping, such as location of local council facility, recycling, etc.

3 Food chains

This chapter covers the following elements of the National Curriculum for Year 4.

Pupils should be taught to:

- construct and interpret a variety of food chains, identifying producers, predators and prey.

It also includes the following elements not mentioned in the National Curriculum:

- how to use food chains to show feeding relationships in a habitat (ISEB 1f)
- how to place organisms in order in a food chain; the terms *producer*, *consumer*, *herbivore*, *carnivore* and *omnivore*; about the relationship between predator and prey (ISEB 1f)
- about how nearly all food chains start with a green plant (ISEB 1g)
- that a food chain represents the transfer of the energy content of food from one organism to another; that the energy is originally from the Sun and converted by plants to food at the start of each food chain (ISEB 1g).

Activities in this chapter offer opportunities to work scientifically by

- asking relevant questions and using different types of scientific enquiries to answer them
- gathering, recording, classifying and presenting data in a variety of ways to help in answering questions
- using results to draw simple conclusions, make predictions for new values, suggest improvements and raise further questions.

Exercise 3.1

1 (a) microscopic plant —is eaten by→ **water flea** —is eaten by→ stickleback

  (b) **pondweed** —is eaten by→ pond snail —is eaten by→ dragonfly larva

  (c) pondweed —is eaten by→ mayfly larva —is eaten by→ **dragonfly larva/stickleback**

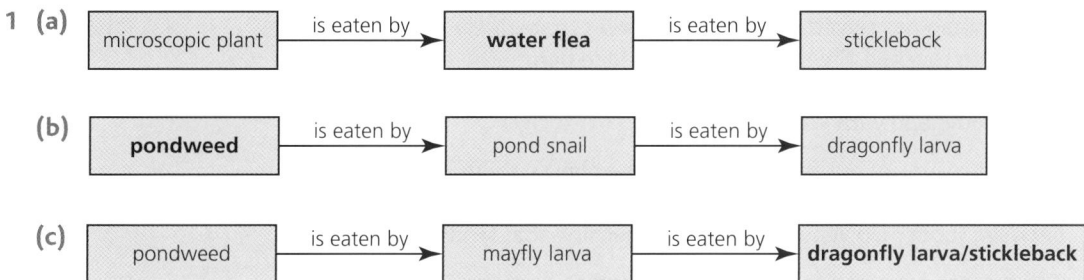

2 Individual answers will need checking against the information in the table. There will need to be at least four organisms in the chain, to include the kingfisher (for example, **microscopic plant** eaten by **water flea** eaten by **stickleback** eaten by **kingfisher**).

Exercise 3.2a

1 Plants are the only living things that can take in energy from the Sun and turn it into food energy.

2 sunlight, water and carbon dioxide

3 A herbivore eats only plants but an omnivore eats plants and other animals/meat.

4 Arrows mean 'is eaten by' (or 'is food for'); the direction of energy flow.

5 An animal that hunts other animals to eat.

6 Eyes on the front of the head allow them to judge distances accurately when hunting.

7 They are prey animals and the eyes on the sides of their head allow them to see all around to watch for predators.

Exercise 3.2b

1 producers, food, photosynthesis

2 energy

3 consumers

4 herbivore

5 carnivores

6 plants, animals

Exercise 3.3: extension

1 These plants are growing in soils that cannot provide enough minerals for healthy growth.

2 Venus flytrap, pitcher plant (other carnivorous plants may be named, e.g. sundew.)

3 The Venus flytrap has sensitive hairs on its leaves that trigger the trap to close when they are touched. (Two touches are needed before the trap is triggered.) Pitcher plants have turned some of their leaves into pitchers (cup shapes) filled with liquid and with very slippery sides.

4 (a) Answers may vary but should focus on the plant's ability to distinguish between the different foods, e.g. can Venus flytraps tell the difference between foods? Do Venus flytraps eat anything that lands on their traps?

   (b) The flytraps appeared to be able to distinguish between the foods and would close more quickly around foods high in protein. They did not respond to sugar solution.

4 Teeth and digestion

This chapter covers the following elements of the National Curriculum for Year 4.

Pupils should be taught to:

- describe the simple functions of the basic parts of the digestive system in humans
- identify the different types of teeth in humans and their simple functions.

It also includes the following elements not mentioned in the National Curriculum:

- about the functions and care of teeth (ISEB 2a)
- the main kinds of teeth (incisors, canines, pre-molars and molars) and their functions; about the effect of bacteria (plaque), fluoride and diet on dental decay; the importance of dental care and hygiene (ISEB 2a)
- the difference between the teeth of carnivores and herbivores (ISEB 2b)
- how to identify skulls of animals with herbivore, carnivore and omnivore diets (ISEB 2b)
- about the simple functions of the basic parts of the digestive system in humans (ISEB 2c)
- about the main parts of the digestive system: mouth, tongue, teeth, esophagus (gullet), stomach, small and large intestine (ISEB 2c).

Activities in this chapter offer opportunities to work scientifically by:

- making systematic and careful observations
- gathering, recording, classifying and presenting data in a variety of ways to help in answering questions
- recording findings using simple scientific language, drawings, labelled diagrams and tables
- identifying differences, similarities or changes related to simple scientific ideas and processes
- reporting on findings from enquiries, including oral and written explanations

Exercise 4.1

Type of tooth	Function
incisors	biting and cutting
molars and pre-molars	**grinding and chewing**
canines	tearing and catching prey

Exercise 4.2a

1 incisors, canines, pre-molars and molars

2 the crown

3 the hard, shiny outer surface of a tooth

4 20

5 32

6 plaque

7 They feed on sugar and turn it into acid. This wears away the tooth to form a cavity.

8 Brush your teeth properly at least twice a day, avoid too many sugary foods and drinks, and visit the dentist regularly.

Exercise 4.2b

1 canines, incisors, molars, pre-molars

2 milk

3 adult

4 bacteria, acid, enamel, cavities

Exercise 4.2c

1 For example: newborn babies are fed with milk from their mother's breasts so they do not need to chew / teeth would make it harder to suckle / teeth would be uncomfortable for/might injure the mother.

2 Responses will need to be assessed individually. The diary entry should show an understanding of the role of brushing in removal of bacteria and how sugars in food feed bacteria. It should also mention that bacteria form acid from sugars and that this creates cavities in which bacteria can hide.

Exercise 4.3a

1 mouth, esophagus (gullet), stomach, small intestine, large intestine

2 (a) stomach

   (b) esophagus (gullet)

   (c) mouth

   (d   small intestine

   (e) large intestine

Exercise 4.3b: extension

Individual responses will need to be checked to ensure that they have the organs in the correct order and show the functions of each correctly.

5 States of matter

This chapter covers the following elements of the National Curriculum for Year 4.

Pupils should be taught to:

- compare and group materials together, according to whether they are solids, liquids or gases
- observe that some materials change state when they are heated or cooled, and measure or research the temperature at which this happens in degrees Celsius (°C)
- identify the part played by evaporation and condensation in the water cycle and associate the rate of evaporation with temperature.

It also includes the following elements not mentioned in the National Curriculum:

- to recognise differences between solids, liquids and gases, in terms of ease of flow and maintenance of shape and volume (ISEB 3a)
- how to use simple particle theory to describe the arrangement of particles in solids, liquids and gases (ISEB 3a)
- to describe changes that occur when materials (e.g. water, clay, dough) are heated or cooled (ISEB 3b)
- that heating or cooling can cause a change of state; the names given to these changes, i.e. *melting*, *boiling*, *condensing*, *evaporating* (ISEB 3b)
- the part played by evaporation and condensation in the water cycle (ISEB 3c)
- how to carry out simple experiments on evaporation and condensation; how these processes relate to the water cycle (ISEB 3c).

Activities in this chapter offer opportunities to work scientifically by:

- setting up simple practical enquiries, comparative and fair tests
- making systematic and careful observations and, where appropriate, taking accurate measurements using standard units, using a range of equipment, including thermometers and dataloggers
- gathering, recording, classifying and presenting data in a variety of ways to help in answering questions
- reporting on findings from enquiries, including oral and written explanations or presentations of results and conclusions
- using results to draw simple conclusions
- identifying differences, similarities or changes related to simple scientific ideas and processes
- using straightforward scientific evidence to answer questions or to support their findings.

Exercise 5.1

1 solid(s), liquid(s), gas(es)

2 compressible

3 solid

4 liquids, gases

5 gases

6 liquid

7 volume (size)

Exercise 5.2a

1 The particles are arranged in a regular pattern and tightly packed together.

2 liquid – particles should be shown close together but not in a regular pattern

gas – particles should be shown spaced widely apart

particles in a liquid   particles in a gas

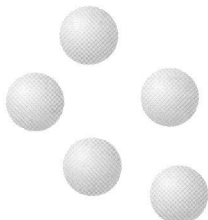

3 The particles in a gas are widely spaced so they can be pushed closer together. The particles in solids and liquids are already very close together so they cannot be pushed closer.

Exercise 5.2b

1 solid

2 far apart

3 vibrate

4 liquid

Exercise 5.2c: extension

Ideas might include: Air is compressible so it will even out the bumps. Metal strips are solid and cannot compress so all the bumps in the road will be felt by the rider. Rubber is flexible so it will allow the tyre to flex as the gas inside is compressed and then released.

Exercise 5.3a

1 freezing

2 0 °C

3 The water turns from a liquid into a gas or vapour.

4 100 °C

5 Water vapour in the air cools on contact with the cold window and condenses into droplets of liquid water.

Exercise 5.3b

1 freezing

2 evaporates, vapour

3 solid, liquid

4 condense

Exercise 5.3c: extension

Give credit for any sensible suggestion, supported by reference to the energy and movement of particles.

The moving particles of air in the wind collide with the water particles in the puddle and knock them out into the air more quickly than would be the case on a still day. Warm particles have more energy than cool ones so the warmth from the Sun will also increase the rate of drying because the energetic air particle will collide more quickly and more often with the water. The warmer, more energetic water particles will stretch and strain the bonds between them and so they are more likely to break.

6 Sound and hearing

This chapter covers the following elements of the National Curriculum for Year 4.

Pupils should be taught to:

- identify how sounds are made, associating some of them with something vibrating
- recognise that vibrations from sounds travel through a medium to the ear
- find patterns between the pitch of a sound and features of the object that produced it
- find patterns between the volume of a sound and the strength of the vibrations that produced it
- recognise that sounds get fainter as the distance from the sound source increases.

It also includes the following elements not mentioned in the National Curriculum:

- how to demonstrate that vibrations are not always visible, e.g. vibrations of a drum skin shown by using rice grains (ISEB 4a)
- that an increase/decrease in the size of the vibration produces a louder/quieter sound, and a faster/slower vibration produces a higher/lower-pitched sound (ISEB 4b)
- that on a stringed instrument, changing the length, tightness and thickness of a string will affect the pitch of a note (ISEB 4b)
- that vibrations from sound sources require a medium (e.g. air, metal, wood, glass) through which to travel to the ear (ISEB 4d)
- that sound travels through solids, liquids and gases but not through a vacuum (ISEB 4d)
- how the ear works; that sound causes the eardrum to vibrate and that different people have different audible ranges (ISEB 4e)
- some effects of loud sounds on the ear (e.g. temporary deafness) (ISEB 4f)
- that loud sounds can cause temporary or permanent damage to hearing (ISEB 4f).

Activities in this chapter offer opportunities to work scientifically by:

- setting up simple practical enquiries, comparative and fair tests
- gathering, recording, classifying and presenting data in a variety of ways to help in answering questions
- reporting on findings from enquiries, including oral and written explanations
- using results to draw simple conclusions, make predictions for new values, suggest improvements and raise further questions
- using straightforward scientific evidence to answer questions or to support their findings.

Exercise 6.1

1 vibrate

2 vibrations

3 strings

4 percussion

5 air, vibrate

Exercise 6.2a

1 Responses will need to be checked individually to make sure that the instruments have been placed in the correct group.

2 volume

3 blow more gently

4 close all the holes

5 play a thinner string, tighten the sting, make the vibrating part of the string shorter by pressing down on it

6 The vibrations are larger so the sound is louder.

Exercise 6.2b

1 (a) lower

(b) quieter

(c) higher

(d) higher

(e) louder

2 (a) volume

(b) pitch

Exercise 6.2c: extension

The strings could be tightened using the tuning pegs until they are tight enough to vibrate properly.

Guitar strings are usually tuned as follows:

- string 1 (thinnest) to E above middle C
- string 2 to B above middle C
- string 3 to G above middle C
- string 4 to D above middle C
- string 5 to A below middle C
- string 6 (thickest) to E below middle C

To achieve this, the notes can be played on a piano or an electronic tuner, and then the tightness of each guitar string is adjusted until the pitch is the same as the reference note.

Exercise 6.3a

1 solids

2 air and the glass in the window

3 Sounds get quieter the further you are from the source.

4 A space that contains absolutely nothing.

5 Because outer space is like a vacuum and sounds cannot travel through a vacuum. (Note: a perfect vacuum is almost impossible to achieve and even outer space contains particles. However, these are so widely dispersed that they are unable to transmit vibrations.)

6 The vibrations in the air make the eardrum vibrate. This makes the small bones in the middle ear vibrate. These vibrations pass to the inner ear where they are detected by nerves, which send the message to the brain.

7 As we get older the nerves in the inner ear become damaged and this reduces the auditory range. It is the ability to hear the higher pitched sounds that is lost first.

8 The large vibrations making a loud sound can damage the eardrum or even tear it. This could cause temporary or permanent deafness.

Exercise 6.3b

1 vibrations

2 liquids, gases, vacuum

3 eardrum

4 brain

5 eardrum, deaf

6 quieter

7 high-pitched

Exercise 6.3c: extension

The squeaks bounce off objects, such as trees and other objects in the environment or flying insects, and the bats detect the reflected sounds with their very sensitive ears. They can tell where the reflected sound comes from and also whether it has been reflected off a hard, solid object, such as a wall or rock, or a softer object, such as a tree. If the object is moving, they can detect the direction and speed of the movement. They can use this information to build up a picture of what is around them so they do not bump into things. They can also detect insects and other prey.

Those studying bats use a bat detector to slow down the vibrations from the squeaks. This lowers the pitch, bringing the sounds into the audible range of an adult. Each species of bat makes a different pattern of squeaks, including differences in pitch and so this can be used to identify which species are present.

7 Electricity

This chapter covers the following elements of the National Curriculum for Year 4.

Pupils should be taught to:

- identify common appliances that run on electricity
- construct a simple series electrical circuit, identifying and naming its basic parts, including cells, wires, bulbs, switches and buzzers
- identify whether or not a bulb will light in a simple series circuit, based on whether or not the bulb is part of a complete loop with a battery
- recognise that a switch opens and closes a circuit and associate this with whether or not a bulb lights in a simple series circuit
- recognise some common conductors and insulators, and associate metals with being good conductors.

It also includes the following elements not mentioned in the National Curriculum:

- how to construct series circuits involving up to three cells, up to three bulbs, a motor, a buzzer and a switch (ISEB 5a)
- that electrical devices will only work if they are part of a complete circuit between the terminals of an electrical supply, and that each part of the circuit must be a conductor of electricity (ISEB 5a)
- the term *in series* (ISEB 5a)
- that metals and carbon (graphite) are conductors of electricity, e.g. copper for household wiring; that most other materials are insulators, e.g. plastic for plug covers (ISEB 5b)
- how to identify common dangers encountered when using electricity and how such dangers are avoided by, for example, the use of insulating materials and fuses (ISEB 5c).

Activities in this chapter offer opportunities to work scientifically by:

- setting up simple practical enquiries and comparative tests
- gathering, recording, classifying and presenting data in a variety of ways to help in answering questions
- recording findings using simple scientific language, drawings, labelled diagrams and tables
- reporting on findings from enquiries, including oral and written explanations, displays or presentations of results and conclusions
- using results to draw simple conclusions, make predictions for new values, suggest improvements and raise further questions
- identifying differences, similarities or changes related to simple scientific ideas and processes
- using straightforward scientific evidence to answer questions or to support their findings.

Exercise 7.1

1   static

2   negative, positive

3   repel

4   attract

Exercise 7.2

1   The positive terminal has a metal button on it and is marked with a '+'. The negative terminal is flat and may be marked with a '−'.

2

3   There must be a complete circuit joining each of the terminals of the bulb to a different terminal of the cell.

4   A   no

   B   yes

   C   no

   D   yes

   E   yes

   F   no

Exercise 7.3a

1   add another cell

2   The two bulbs are sharing the energy from the one cell.

3   Connect the material into a circuit with a cell and a bulb. If the bulb lights up, the material is an electrical conductor. If the bulb does not light up, the material is an electrical insulator.

4   Becky is right. All metals are electrical conductors. Most non-metals are insulators but graphite is a non-metal that conducts electricity.

5   It opens and closes a gap in the circuit. When the gap is closed, the electricity can flow so the components work. When the gap is open the electricity cannot flow.

Exercise 7.3b

1 conductors

2 insulators

3 conductors

4 graphite

5 brightly

6 dimly

7 switch

Exercise 7.4a

1 dangerous

2 damaged

3 plug

4 water

5 plastic, insulator

6 fuse, break

Exercise 7.4b: extension

This will need individual assessment and can be used to support literacy speaking and listening targets. The talk should outline the basic safety rules for using electricity and explain the reasons for them clearly. If a poster or slides are used to illustrate the talk, they should be clear and contain appropriate images that support the content of the talk.